Stop Here! Remarkable Roadside Attractions

BY LISA TRUMBAUER

CONTENTS

Celebration Press
Pearson Learning Group

ROADS, ROADS EVERYWHERE!

Take a look at a road map of the United States. What do you see? Hundreds and hundreds of highways and roads. They run from the Atlantic Ocean to the Pacific Ocean. They run from Canada to Mexico. Roads lead you north, south, east, and west—and everywhere in between!

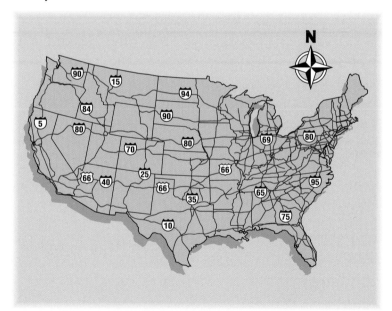

Highways crisscross the United States.

Americans are constantly on the go. They travel to and from work. They visit friends and family in different cities and different states. Sometimes people jump into the car and drive, just to see interesting new places and things. You have probably taken some long car trips with your family.

It wasn't always like this, however. One hundred years ago the United States looked very different. Although early versions of the automobile existed, their use was not widespread. They were still too expensive for the average person to afford.

Also there weren't many **paved roads** at that time. Roads that did exist certainly didn't resemble today's wide, crowded highways. Unpaved roads seemed fine for riding short distances on horseback or traveling by horse and buggy. If people wanted to travel far, they could take a train.

Travel was difficult on unpaved roads. Vehicles could easily get stuck in the mud.

Then, in 1908, Henry Ford began to manufacture his legendary automobile, the Model T, using the **assembly line.** For the first time there was a car that the average American could afford, and Americans eagerly took to the open road! Traveling was difficult, though, because of poor road conditions.

In 1916 the U.S. government passed the Federal Aid Road Act. It made money available to the states to build roads and to choose where the roads should go. In 1921 the government added to the Road Act. It specified the need for national roads that connected the states, and it increased aid for such highways.

Smart business owners realized that travelers would need three things along the road—gasoline, food, and lodging. Soon gas stations, restaurants, and motels cropped up to meet the travelers' demands. (Did you know that the word *motel* is a blend of *motor* and *hotel*?)

Another type of business also began to appear—unusual roadside attractions. These attractions invited travelers to stop and be entertained by everything from giant sculptures of vegetables to gift shops shaped like prehistoric animals. Traveling became an adventure, and the roadside attractions made it fun.

This gas station offered a free chicken with every fill.

STOP HERE!

By the 1950s it seemed that almost everyone in America had an automobile, and more and more cars crowded the nation's roads. Large **interstate highways** allowed travelers to bypass the smaller, two-lane roads and their quirky roadside attractions for the sake of speed and convenience.

But American roads still do have some wacky sights to marvel over, and people even go out of their way to see them. Take the observation tower called the Sombrero Tower, for example.

The Sombrero Tower, an observation tower that is part of the South of the Border attraction

©roadsideamerica.com, Kirby, Smith & Wilkins

You can see it from Interstate 95 in South Carolina, just south of the North Carolina border. Almost 200 feet tall, it's part of South of the Border, an enormous tourist attraction that provides everything that travelers need—gas, food, lodging, and fun!

At South of the Border, you can get Mexican food, play a round of miniature golf, and fill your gas tank. If a good night's sleep is what you need, you can find plenty of motel rooms. You can even get married there!

A man named Alan Schafer created this roadside attraction, which began as a small beverage stand in the 1950s. When he gave people directions to his stand, he usually included the phrase "just south of the border" (the North Carolina border, that is). To take advantage of the Mexican flavor of these directions, Schafer renamed his stand and started selling Mexican **souvenirs** there. His business has been growing ever since.

For Fish Fanatics

Have you ever had a burning desire to stand inside the mouth of a fish? Maybe not, but this roadside attraction can give you an idea of what it might feel like!

The funny fish shown here is actually part of a museum. The National Freshwater Fishing Hall of Fame was founded in 1970 in Hayward, Wisconsin. Freshwater fishing and water sports are popular in the Hayward area. In the main museum building, you can view displays of old fishing reels, tackle boxes, and boat motors. The museum's crowning achievement, however, is its giant **muskie.** A muskie is—what else?—a fish.

©roadsideamerica.com, Kirby, Smith & Wilkins

Real muskies are usually between 3 and 4 feet long. This greenish-colored muskie, however, is bigger than most. The giant fiberglass statue is 143 feet long and stands four and one-half stories high! Visitors can enter the muskie's belly through a door, walk inside its body, and stand on an observation deck under its large teeth inside its wide-open mouth.

MN

2

Hayward

WI

The muskie is part of the Hall of Fame's sculpture garden, which also includes other fiberglass fish statues. If you are passing through Wisconsin on Routes 63 or 27, keep an eye out for the giant muskie!

The huge fiberglass muskie statue at the National Freshwater Fishing Hall of Fame

9

Models of two enormous dinosaurs tower over the landscape at the Wheel Inn in Cabazon, California.

DiNOSAUR DRiVE-BYS

Imagine you're driving down Interstate 10 near Cabazon, California, when suddenly you see a startling image from the past. Two huge dinosaurs rise up alongside you, seemingly out of nowhere.

Models of dinosaurs have dotted American roads for many years. These two creatures were the brainchild of Claude Belle, the owner of the Wheel Inn. One dinosaur is an **Apatosaurus.** A small museum and souvenir shop reside in its belly. The other, a **Tyrannosaurus rex,** boasts a giant slide for children down its tail.

Dinosaur attractions are not limited to California. Vernal, Utah, once called itself the "Dinosaur Capital of the World." Nearby, travelers can view large numbers of **fossilized** dinosaur bones inside the Dinosaur National Monument. Just outside the national park, dinosaur-themed motels and restaurants run all along Route 40.

Other fun places to spot dino dynamos are Prehistoric Land, just off Interstate 94 in Wisconsin Dells, Wisconsin, and Dinosaur World in Beaver, Arkansas.

GIANT FOLK HERO

Two of the largest figures in American **folklore** are Paul Bunyan and his blue ox, Babe. It's only fitting, then, that Paul and Babe have been immortalized in some of the tallest roadside attractions in the United States.

The first town to build large statues of Paul and Babe was Bemidji (buh MIH jee), Minnesota. Bemidji is a small logging town

Statues of Paul Bunyan and his blue ox, Babe, in Bemidji, Minnesota

along Route 2. The townspeople of Bemidji must have related to Paul

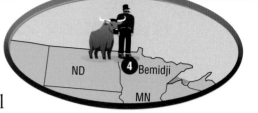

Bunyan, who could cut down trees an acre at a time. The statues in Bemidji were built in 1937.

Other towns in Minnesota, such as Brainerd, on Route 371, have also built enormous statues of Paul and Babe. If you want to get your picture taken with Paul, be sure to stop by the town of Akeley on Route 34. Here a 25-foot Paul holds his palm outstretched for you to sit in.

Klamath, California, also honors Paul Bunyan and Babe with statues of each. These statues tower over the cars that zoom past them on U.S. Highway 101. They mark the entrance to Trees of Mystery, a tourist attraction of strangely shaped trees among the California redwoods.

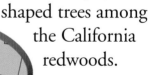

BiG CHAiR CHALLENGE

If Paul Bunyan really were as huge as the legends and statues honoring him suggest, perhaps he might have had use for one of these—the world's largest chairs.

If you drive along Interstate 81 or Interstate 88 through Binghamton, New York, you will see what was once the largest chair ever built. It stands 24 feet and 9 inches tall, and its seat measures 12 feet across.

The huge chair was built in the 1970s to outdo other chairs claimed to be the "world's largest." It even made *The Guinness Book of World Records* in 1979 as the largest chair in the world.

The first large chair was constructed in 1905 in Gardner, Massachusetts. Townspeople thought it would call attention to the furniture industry in the area. The chair was 12 feet tall. In 1922 a 13-foot 6-inch chair was built in Thomasville, North Carolina. It was replaced in 1951 with an 18-foot chair on a 12-foot base.

©roadsideamerica.com, Kirby, Smith & Wilkins

This giant Duncan Phyfe-style chair in Thomasville, North Carolina, represents the city's furniture industry.

The competition heated up! About five towns, all proud of their furniture products, wanted to build the largest chair. In 1999 the largest chair was reported to be in Los Angeles, California. It towered over 53 feet tall and could supposedly survive earthquakes and 70-mile-per-hour winds.

Who knows where the next giant chair will show up!

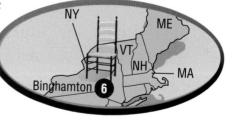

HAVING A BALL

What does a **gargantuan** ball of twine look like? If you drive through Darwin, Minnesota, or Cawker City, Kansas (near Concordia), you can see for yourself. You'll have to get off the main highways, though.

Francis A. Johnson created the first of these massive balls. It weighed 17,400 pounds and measured about 40 feet around. The ball is on display in the Darwin city park off Route 12.

Frances A. Johnson displays his massive ball of twine.

Frank Stoeber of Cawker City, Kansas, decided in 1953 to try to beat this record. His ball used over a million feet of twine. When Stoeber passed away in 1974, the ball measured 11 feet around, and it's still growing! Every year the people of Cawker City have a "twine-a-thon," when they add more twine. In this way the ball keeps growing. Travelers can see it in the middle of town in an open-air shelter.

Neither of these balls is the largest, however. According to *The Guinness Book of World Records,* J.C. Payne of Valley View, Texas, made the largest ball of string. Between 1989 and 1991 he rolled a ball of colored nylon twine measuring just over 41 feet around. You can see it at Ripley's Believe It or Not Museum in Branson, Missouri. This record may not last, however. Someone may be working on the world's next largest ball of twine right now!

THAT'S NUTS!

Many roadside attractions call attention to community pride. This is especially true of those representing products made or grown locally. For example, in Gaffney, South Carolina, there is a huge peach-shaped water tower. The town of Strawberry Point, Iowa, erected a 15-foot-tall strawberry. You can see an 11-foot-tall egg in Winlock, Washington.

One of the largest of the large is in Brunswick, Missouri, along Route 24. In 1982, George and Elizabeth James, who owned a pecan farm, built an enormous pecan out of concrete. The 12,000-pound structure represents a particular kind of thin-shelled pecan that they discovered and cultivated. The concrete pecan is 12 feet long and 7 feet wide.

This enormous sculpture in Brunswick, Missouri, represents a giant variety of pecan grown in the state.

The peanut also has its supporters. In Pearsall, Texas, a sign boasts, "PEARSALL, TEXAS/ WORLD'S LARGEST PEANUT/55,000,000 LBS. MARKETED ANNUALLY." On top of the sign is a peanut, 6 feet long.

The state of Georgia should not be left out. After all, the peanut is one of its most important crops. Standing on top of a 15-foot-tall pillar in Ashburn, Georgia, off Interstate 55 is a 10-foot-long peanut.

CAR CRUSADE

One of the first major highways built in the United States was Route 66. Stretching more than 2,400 miles, it started in Chicago and ended in Los Angeles. Begun in 1926, Route 66 connected the midwestern United States with the West Coast.

More modern highways have since replaced many parts of Route 66. Other parts run along near newer highways. In Texas, Interstate 40 is now the road of choice. But from I-40 just outside Amarillo, travelers can see one man's tribute to Route 66, the automobile, and the traveler's desire to head west.

Cadillac Ranch off Interstate 40
near Amarillo, Texas